JUDGE JUDY SHEINDLIN'S

You Can't Judge a Book
by Its Cover

JUDGE JUDY SHEINDLIN'S

You Can't Judge a Book by Its Cover

Cool Rules for School

ILLUSTRATED BY BOB TORE

Cliff Street Books
An Imprint of HarperCollins*Publishers*
www.harperchildrens.com

Judge Judy Sheindlin's You Can't Judge a Book by Its Cover
Text copyright © 2001 by Judge Judy Sheindlin
Illustrations copyright © 2001 by Bob Tore
Printed in the U.S.A. All rights reserved.
www.harperchildrens.com

Library of Congress Cataloging-in-Publication Data is available.

ISBN 0-06-029483-3 — ISBN 0-06-029484-1 (lib. bdg.)
Typography by Matt Adamec
1 2 3 4 5 6 7 8 9 10
❖
First Edition

This book is dedicated to our grandchildren—
Casey, Taylor, and Jenna, who go to school now,
and Sarah, Jake, Abraham, and Alexei, who will go to school soon.

Calm before the storm

Variety is the spice of life

Put the cart before the horse

No use beating a dead horse   Dirt cheap

I have other fish to fry   Leave no stone unturned

That takes the cake

Where there's smoke there's fire

Never a borrower or a lender be

Face the music

Easier said than done

The early bird catches the worm   Handwriting is on the wall

Rob Peter to pay Paul

Make hay white the sun shines   Practice what you preach

Jack of all trades and a master of none

You made your bed now you must lie in it   Keep your head above water

No defense like a good offense   Say what you mean and mean what you say

No man can serve two masters

Hand to mouth   shot in the dark   Penny wise and pound foolish

You can't teach an old dog new tricks   Water over the dam

Virtue is its own reward

You get what you pay for   Practice makes perfect

paddle your own canoe   Nothing ventured nothing gained

Get one's goat

A fool and his money are soon parted

To the Kids

Adults seem to have little sayings for everything. But what do they really mean? They sound very interesting, but how do you use them in your everyday life to solve problems and make the right choices?

All of you will go to school for at least twelve years. Many of you will go on to college and some of you to professional school. The subjects that you will learn will help prepare you for a good job and to be a smart person. Growing up to be a good, kind, caring, honest, and responsible person is just as important.

In this book you will find some of those interesting little adult sayings. They are explained using problems that all kids face in school. It is your job to choose the best answer to the problem.

Talk about the answers with your parents and friends. Then take those wise little sayings and make them part of your vocabulary.

When you grow up, you can pass them on to your children.

Have fun with the book. Make up some of your own answers. Make up some of your own problems. But most of all—make the right choices.

Judy Sheindlin

Don't bite off more than you can chew

You agreed to take care of your teacher's new litter of puppies for the day. After an hour, you realize how much work it really is.

You should:

A. Do the best you can until the teacher comes home.

B. Ask a friend to help you.

C. Try to get your mother to watch them.

D. Hold a puppy sale.

If you don't have anything nice to say, don't say anything at all

Your best friend's cousin is visiting and wants you to go skating after school, but she seems to be a bit goofy.

You should:

A. Tell your friend you wouldn't be caught dead with her.

B. Fake being sick to get out of it.

C. Go along with her; maybe she is really nice.

D. Buy her a mask.

Sticks and stones may break my bones, but words will never harm me

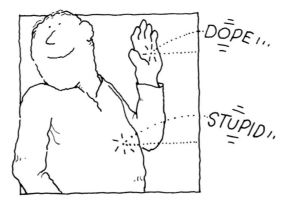

Your father is driving you to school, and the car in front of your father's car just cut him off. The driver shouts something nasty, and your father speeds up to catch him.

You should:

A. Tell your father that you're going to tell your mother if he doesn't stop.

B. Tell your father to hit the gas because this is very exciting.

C. Tell your father to forget it, because the other guy is a jerk and it's stupid to get into an accident.

D. Ask your father to stop and call the police.

Don't make a mountain out of a molehill

You're at the baseball game and one of your friends
just struck out, costing your school the championship.
A bunch of kids are screaming terrible things at him.

You should:

A. Yell at the kids to stop because they're being cruel.

B. Start screaming too—he deserves it.

C. Tell your friend not to feel bad; it's only a game.

D. Suggest he needs batting practice and you'll help him.

You can't judge a book by its cover

It's the first day of school and your teacher looks very tough.

You should:

A. Give him a hard time because you think he's going to give you a hard time.

B. Try to get out of his class.

C. Be extra well behaved; maybe he'll like you.

D. Give him a chance; maybe he's really nice.

Never put off until tomorrow what you can do today

The teacher is looking at you, and you know that any minute he is going to call on you to give a book report. But you didn't read the book, and your mind is a complete blank.

You should:

A. Raise your hand and tell the teacher you have to go to the bathroom.

B. Raise your hand and ask him if you can have another day to prepare.

C. Avoid all eye contact with the teacher.

D. Make up an excuse and hope he's not paying attention.

When the cat's away, the mice will play

Today you have a substitute teacher. Whenever that happens, the class gets very wild.

You should:

A. Ask permission to go to the bathroom and head to the mall.

B. Do what you want because the teacher doesn't even know your name.

C. Not behave like a baby—maybe you will learn something special from the teacher.

D. Throw your best spitball.

If the shoe fits, wear it

Your teacher just told you that the principal would like to see you in his office after class.

You should:

A. Tell the principal that the teacher made a mistake and you're the wrong person.

B. Ask the teacher to let you off the hook because you're scared.

C. Accept responsibility for what you did.

D. Quit school.

Anything worth doing is worth doing well

You're struggling with your math homework, and you're having a tough time understanding it.

You should:

A. Call a friend for the answers.

B. Take your time and try to understand it.

C. Ask your parents to help.

D. Write down any old answers, even if they are wrong.

Better safe than sorry

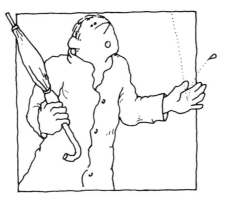

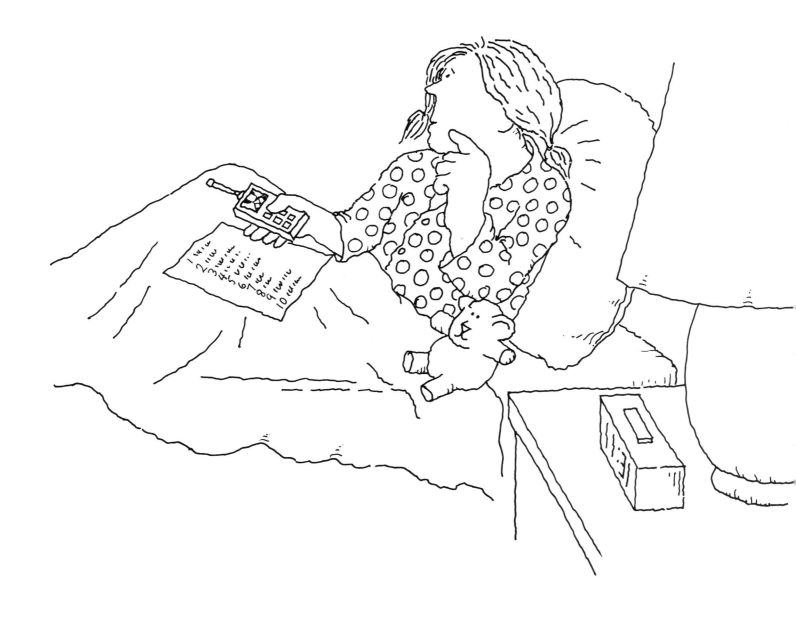

You just finished your homework that's due in the morning. You answered the ten questions you were supposed to—or was it twenty questions? It's too late to call anybody and ask.

You should:

A. Forget about it and go to sleep. It was probably ten questions.

B. Tell the teacher that you misunderstood her.

C. Tell the teacher that you lost half of your homework on the way to school.

D. Do the other ten and get a good night's sleep.

The squeaky wheel gets the grease

You really have to go to the bathroom. You've had your hand raised for a long time, and you think the teacher is ignoring you.

You should:

A. Continue to try and catch her eye. If she doesn't see you, call her name.

B. If you can't wait, just go to the bathroom before you have an accident.

C. Quietly get out of your seat and explain your problem to the teacher.

D. Stand up and hop from foot to foot doing the wee-wee dance.

A friend in need is a friend indeed

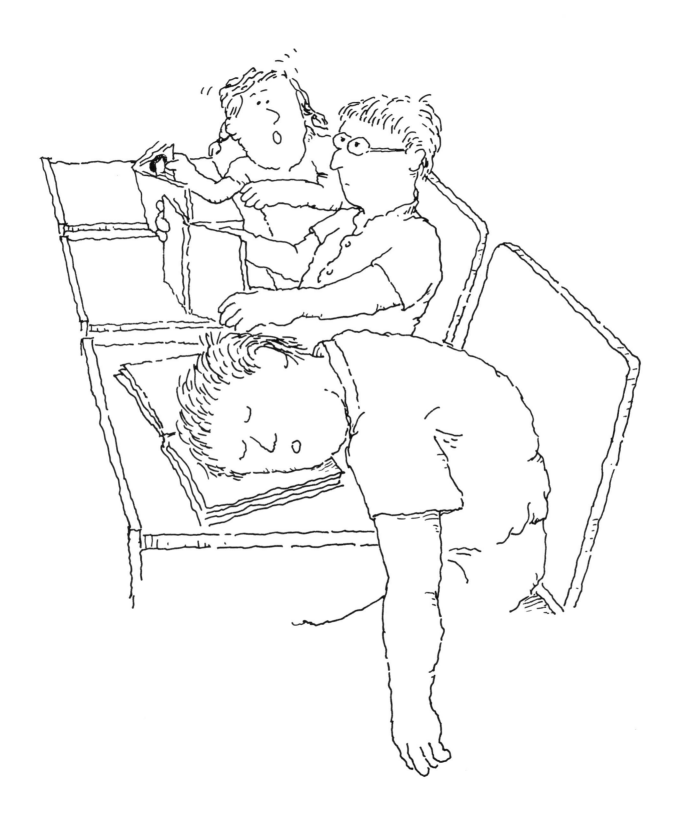

A good friend of yours is sitting a couple of desks away. He keeps falling asleep while the teacher is talking.

You should:

A. Whisper his name when the teacher turns around.

B. Try throwing an eraser at him.

C. Mind your own business and let him sleep.

D. Roll up a notebook and whack him on the head.

Two wrongs don't make a right

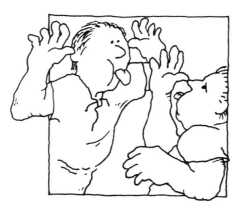

The salami sandwich that your mother prepared for you is missing from your lunch box. You suspect one of your friends took it because he smells like salami.

You should:

A. Ask him if he saw your sandwich.

B. Take his lunch box and search it.

C. Steal his lunch.

D. Tell him your sandwich smells like salami but really is dog food.

Step up and face the music

Your report card is really bad. The last thing you need now is to have to show it to your father.

You should:

A. Show it to him and promise to try harder.

B. Show it to your father when he's half-asleep; maybe he won't read it too carefully.

C. Sign his name to the report card and hope the teacher accepts it.

D. Add a plus sign to every grade.

It's not whether you win or lose, but how you play the game

Your team just lost a basketball game to a visiting team. You're the team captain. The other captain comes to shake your hand.

You should:

A. Ignore him because you're in a lousy mood.

B. Shake his hand and be a good sport.

C. Accuse him of winning by cheating.

D. Stick out your foot and trip him.

Keep your hands to yourself

A boy in your class is touching you in a very personal way.

You should:

A. Tell him to stop and immediately tell the teacher.

B. Walk away and say nothing.

C. Start screaming and yelling as loud as you can until someone notices.

D. Make him stop, tell the teacher, and then tell your parents as soon as you get home.

Do unto others as you would have others do unto you

It's the first day back at school, and there's a new kid sitting alone on the bus.

You should:

A. Sit with all your friends; that's where the fun is.

B. Invite him to join you and your friends.

C. Sit next to him and make him feel welcome.

D. Just ignore him; you don't owe him a thing.

Curiosity killed the cat

Your teacher gives you a note in a sealed envelope for your parents. You're afraid the note is about your poor conduct.

You should:

A. Stick the sealed envelope under a pile of papers on your father's desk.

B. Don't open it. You'll probably get in a lot of trouble.

C. Give your parents the envelope and hope they are in a good mood.

D. Steam it open.

One rotten apple can spoil the whole barrel

A bully is threatening to hurt you if you don't steal something for him.

You should:

A. Steal it and then tell the teacher the bully has it.

B. Do what he says so you won't get hurt.

C. Tell the teacher and your parents about the threat.

D. Give him something that you own so that you don't have to steal anything.

Honesty is the best policy

Someone is taking money from your friend's backpack.

You should:

A. Tell the teacher.

B. Try to talk him out of it.

C. Tell him you want half of the money or you'll call the police.

D. Send him an unsigned note telling him that you know what he did and he should put the money back.

Beware of the wolf in sheep's clothing

You are playing in the schoolyard and a strange man calls you over to him. He says he wants to ask you a question.

You should:

A. Walk away with your friends.

B. Try being friendly—maybe he's lost.

C. Don't go near him but ask him what he wants.

D. Walk away and go get the teacher immediately.

Practice makes perfect

You handed in your cursive writing assignment, and the teacher is having trouble reading it.

You should:

A. Ask your teacher to clean his glasses.

B. Explain that you didn't have time to do the assignment and you had to finish it on the bus. It's not your fault that the ride was bumpy.

C. Offer to do the assignment over.

D. Accept the teacher's criticism and do a better job next time.